EXPLORING EARTH'S · BIOMES ·

CORAL REEF

APRIL PULLEY SAYRE

TFCB

TWENTY-FIRST CENTURY BOOKS

A Division of Henry Holt and Company
• New York •

For Uncle Tom and Aunt Veda,
our Caribbean compatriots.

ACKNOWLEDGMENTS

Our thanks to the following experts, who reviewed portions of this manuscript: Michael Rigsby of the Monterey Bay Aquarium and DeeVon Quirolo of Reef Relief.

Twenty-First Century Books
A Division of Henry Holt and Company, Inc.
115 West 18th Street
New York, NY 10011

Henry Holt® and colophon are trademarks of
Henry Holt and Company, Inc.
Publishers since 1866

Text copyright © 1996 by April Pulley Sayre
Illustrations © 1996 by Martha Weston
All rights reserved.
Published in Canada by Fitzhenry & Whiteside Ltd.
195 Allstate Parkway, Markham, Ontario L3R 4T8

Reef Relief ® is a registered trademark of Reef Relief Inc.,
a private nonprofit conservation group dedicated to preserving
and protecting the living coral reef of the Florida Keys.

Library of Congress Cataloging-in-Publication Data
Sayre, April Pulley.
Coral Reef / April Pulley Sayre.—1st ed.
p.   cm.—(Exploring earth's biomes)
Includes bibliographical references (p.   ) and index.
Summary: Describes the physical features of a coral reef,
its community of plants and animals, and environmental threats.
1. Coral reef ecology—Juvenile literature. 2. Coral reefs and islands—Juvenile
literature. [1. Coral reefs and islands. 2. Coral reef ecology. 3. Ecology.]
I Title. II Series: Sayre, April Pulley. Exploring earth's biomes.
QH541.5.C7S3966 1996
574.9′1-dc20   96-2838
                                                              CIP
                                                              AC

B+T 11|97 16.98/13.58

ISBN 0–8050–4087–0
First Edition—1996

Cover design by Betty Lew
Interior design by Kelly Soong

Printed in Mexico
All first editions are printed on acid-free paper ∞.
1 3 5 7 9 10 8 6 4 2

Photo credits appear on page 80.

CONTENTS

INTRODUCTION TO AQUATIC BIOMES

The water that makes up more than two-thirds of your body weight, that flows in your blood, that bathes your cells, and that you cry as tears, may once have flowed in a river. It may have floated as a cloud, fallen as a snowflake, bobbed in ocean waves, or been drunk by a dinosaur from an ancient lake. All this is possible because the water that's presently on earth has always been here—except for ice brought by comets hitting the earth's atmosphere. And all the water on earth is connected in a global cycle. This cycle is called the water cycle, or the hydrologic cycle.

Every day, all over the earth, water exists in and moves through this cycle. Ninety-seven percent of the earth's water is in the oceans. Two percent is in frozen glaciers and ice caps at the Poles. The remaining 1 percent is divided among the world's lakes, rivers, groundwater, soil moisture, and water vapor in the air. All this comes to a grand total of 326 million cubic miles (1,359 million cubic kilometers) of water. Every day, this water is exchanged among the oceans, streams, clouds, glaciers, lakes, wetlands, and even dew-covered leaves. Even now, it is being exhaled from your body, as moisture in your breath.

As the water cycles, at times it changes phase from solid to liquid to gas. The heat of the sun warms water on the land's surface, in lakes, in streams, in the ocean, even on the leaves of plants—and causes this water to evaporate, to turn into a gas. This gas rises into the air, cools, and condenses, eventually forming clouds and falling back to earth as liquid rain or solid snow or hail. This precipitation makes its way into streams, rivers, lakes, oceans, glaciers, and ice caps, and underground. And so the cycle continues. But it's not quite so simple. Each portion of the cycle is connected to others. For example, river water runs into oceans, stream water runs into lakes, and water from underground bubbles out of springs and into rivers. Water is constantly being exchanged among all the many places it resides on planet earth.

Almost anywhere water exists as a liquid, it is colonized by organisms—bacteria, amoebas, fungi, animals, or plants. Some watery habitats have particular physical conditions and particular kinds of plants and animals inhabiting them. These are aquatic biomes: ocean, river, lake, and coral reef. Where these aquatic biomes mingle with terrestrial, or land, biomes, they may form special, semiaquatic, fringe communities. Wetland and seashore are two of these communities that are unique enough and widespread enough to qualify as major biomes.

All aquatic and semiaquatic biomes—ocean, river, lake, coral reef, seashore, and wetland—are influenced by regional climate and the lands nearby. These biomes are also linked to one another, by ever-moving water molecules and the global water cycle through which they flow.

☆ 1 ☆
THE CORAL REEF BIOME

Put on a snorkel and mask, and jump into a warm, tropical ocean. Explore a coral reef. You'll be in for a treat. Nowhere else can you encounter animals so closely and comfortably in their own natural habitat. Colorful fish swim inches away from your face and eye you through your mask. Schools of small squid may hover near your toes, then dart away, flashing colors as they go. A moray eel may poke its head out of a crevice, or a stingray might glide by, like a bird. If you're lucky, you may even see a sea turtle paddling along almost effortlessly, despite its heavy shell.

Coral reefs are a little like underwater cities that rise up from shallow ocean floor. Their "buildings"—their structure—are created by corals. Corals are animals that produce limestone as they grow. Billions of these flowerlike corals live atop limestone that they and their ancestors have formed over thousands of years. Tiny algae "partners" living inside the coral help feed the coral and form the limestone. So coral reefs are the result of a special partnership between coral (an animal) and algae (a plant).

Like a city, a coral reef is busy with inhabitants. A coral reef's mounds, branches, and layers provide surfaces where animals can settle and cracks where they can hide. Sponges grow attached to the reef. Lobsters and worms hide in crevices. Schools of colorful fish circle coral mounds. Cowries—relatives of snails—slowly move along the flat surfaces of coral fans. Damselfish, like underwater gardeners, tend short, green algae lawns. Above the reef, silvery barracudas patrol, looking for small fish to eat.

Like desert and tropical rain forest, coral reef is a biome—an area that has a certain kind of community of animals and plants. It also has a characteristic climate. It only occurs in warm, shallow, tropical or subtropical oceans, where the average temperature of the coldest month is at least 75°F (24°C). This need for a particular climate sets coral reef apart from other aquatic biomes, such as ocean, river, and lake. These biomes can exist in both cold and warm parts of the world. Coral reefs, in contrast, require a very specific climate and can be killed by unusually warm or cold weather.

Coral reefs are concentrated in four main ocean regions: the Indo-Pacific region, the West Indian region, the Eastern Pacific region, and the West African region. The richest coral reefs, with the greatest number of animal species, are found in the Indo-Pacific, which includes the Indian Ocean and western Pacific Ocean. This area encompasses the remarkable Indonesian and Philippine reefs, the Red Sea, and the world's longest expanse of coral reef: the Great Barrier Reef of Australia. The West Indian region is where you'll find the reefs of the Florida Keys and the Caribbean islands. These reefs have fewer species than the Indo-Pacific reefs but possess a beauty all their own. The third main region, the Eastern Pacific, contains the reefs along the west coast of Central and South America, such as the Galápagos reefs. The West African region, along the west coast of Africa, has only a few small reefs and relatively few animal species.

*The coral reefs of the Red Sea are
remarkably diverse—and quite beautiful.*

Coral reefs are often called the tropical rain forests of the ocean. They're special places, with an extremely high diversity—number of different kinds—of animals. Like rain forests, coral reefs are also a strange combination of durability and sensitivity. Parrot fish can chew on them, hurricanes can topple them, yet coral reefs can still recover. But reefs, like rain forests, are vulnerable to a host of environmental threats. For this reason, many people are working to understand coral reefs better and to solve the problems facing this remarkable biome.

CORAL REEF AT A GLANCE

TYPES

There are three main types of coral reefs:
- Fringing reefs—reefs that form a fringe, or edge, around the shore of an island or continent.
- Barrier reefs—reefs that are close to but separated from the shore by quiet waters called lagoons.
- Atolls—large ring-shaped reefs that occur in the open ocean.

DIVISIONS

Coral reefs are divided into four main zones, according to their exposure to ocean waves. The zones are:
- Lagoon—the open water area that separates reef from land.
- Reef flat—the flat or gently sloping area that runs from the beach or lagoon to the crest of the reef. This area has sand, mud, scattered grasses, and coral clumps.
- Reef crest—the highest part of the reef, where waves break.
- Reef front or fore-reef—the front of the reef, which is farthest from the land and farthest out at sea. The reef front may descend like a wall into deeper water.

PHYSICAL FEATURES

- Coral reefs are found in ocean waters that have a water temperature of at least 75°F (24°C) in the coldest month.
- Coral reefs grow near the ocean's surface, in clear waters 6 to 100 feet (1.8 to 30 meters) deep.
- Coral reefs grow mainly in the tropics, from the Tropic of Cancer to the Tropic of Capricorn.
- Reef-building corals need very specific living conditions. They need clear, clean water. They can be killed by water

that is too low in salinity, too muddy, too warm, or too cold, or by exposure to the drying air or too much sunlight.

ANIMALS

- Coral reefs are made by colonies of animals called corals.
- The flesh of reef-building corals contains zooxanthellae—single-celled algae.
- Corals are divided into two types: reef-building corals, which are also called hard corals; and non-reef building corals, such as soft corals, black corals, thorny corals, and horny corals.
- Coral reefs have an extremely high animal diversity. Many of these animals are brightly colored.
- Coral reefs contain more species of fish than any other biome on earth.
- Mollusks, corals, worms, shrimp, sea anemones, sponges, and fish such as eels and manta rays are some of the coral reef's residents.
- Many coral reef animals are involved in symbiotic relationships—close relationships with animals or plants of other species in which at least one of the partners benefits.

PLANTS

- Algae live not only inside corals but on the reef surface as well. Algae grow in many forms, including coatings like green frosting and threadlike filaments like grass lawns. Large algae are called seaweeds.
- Ocean plants such as algae and seaweeds gain the minerals and water they need directly from seawater.
- Plants such as seaweeds and other algae live in shallow parts of the reef, where sunlight is available for photosynthesis. Sea grasses and eelgrasses often cover the ocean floor near the reef.
- Calcareous algae live on the reef and cement the coral together, making the reef sturdier.

☆ 2 ☆
CORAL REEFS OF THE CARIBBEAN AND THE GULF OF MEXICO

The Gulf of Mexico and the Caribbean Sea are bordered by North America, Central America, and South America. These bodies of water are connected to one another and to the Atlantic Ocean. Together they contain about 14 percent of the world's coral reefs.

These reefs are home to colorful corals and strange sponges, plus lobsters, squid, octopi, stingrays, and numerous other fish. Yet they have only about 80 species of coral and 520 fish species, many fewer than Indo-Pacific reefs, which have 600 coral species and more than 2,000 kinds of fish. Nevertheless, the Gulf of Mexico and the Caribbean contain many spectacular reefs. These reefs are popular spots for fishing, snorkeling, and scuba diving.

Structurally, the reefs of the Caribbean are mostly fringing reefs and patch reefs, unlike the atolls that are so common in the Pacific Ocean. Belize, in Central America, has a large barrier reef, second in size only to Australia's Great Barrier Reef. Caribbean coral reefs grow side by side with coastal mangrove swamps and underwater sea grass beds where Caribbean manatees—an endangered mammal—feed.

The Gulf of Mexico has relatively few reefs, other than

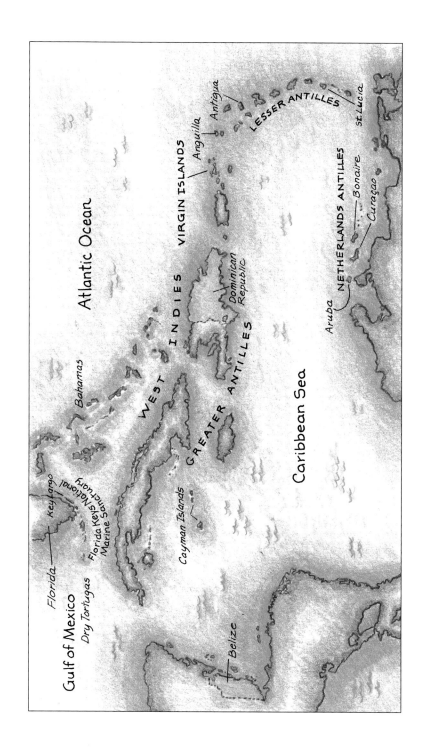

Gulf of Mexico

Atlantic Ocean

Caribbean Sea

Florida

Dry Tortugas

Key Largo

Florida Keys
National Marine Sanctuary

Bahamas

WEST INDIES

GREATER ANTILLES

Cayman Islands

Belize

Dominican Republic

VIRGIN ISLANDS

Anguilla

Antigua

LESSER ANTILLES

St. Lucia

NETHERLANDS ANTILLES

Bonaire

Curaçao

Aruba

the reefs of the Florida Keys. Mud carried into the Gulf by the Mississippi River smothers corals before they begin to form reefs in the shallows. However, a few rocky domes of salt under waters off the coast of Texas do support coral reefs. Farther from the Mississippi, coral reefs border Mexico, near Veracruz, Campeche, and Cozumel.

The Caribbean Sea contains most of the coral reefs close to the United States. Beginning near Florida and curving gently southward toward South America are the West Indies, a group of islands that separates the Atlantic Ocean from the Caribbean Sea. More than a thousand islands are considered part of this island group. The islands have sizable coral reefs and are popular destinations for snorkelers and divers. Many of the West Indies are the tops of extinct underwater volcanoes. Some are mountainous and clothed in green rain forest; other islands are flat, dry, and relatively bare of plants, except for cacti and coconut palms.

The islands of the West Indies are divided into four main groups: the Bahamas, the Greater Antilles, the Lesser Antilles, and the Netherlands Antilles. Part of the West Indies is Bermuda, a small island out in the Atlantic Ocean. Strangely enough, Bermuda is at the same latitude as Beaufort, South Carolina, yet it still has coral reefs. The Gulf Stream, an ocean current, warms Bermuda's waters so much that reef-building corals can grow there.

Here are some of the more interesting features of the coral reefs in the Caribbean and the Gulf of Mexico:

- The 3,707-square-mile (9,638-square-kilometer) Florida Keys National Marine Sanctuary protects the world's third largest barrier reef, the Florida Keys. The sanctuary stretches from Key Largo to the Dry Tortugas, in the Gulf of Mexico. Near Key Largo, scientists can study coral reefs by spending several weeks living in the Aquarius Under-

Sea fans like these are a type of soft coral found in the Florida Keys.

water laboratory, 62 feet (18.9 meters) below the ocean's surface.

- Just offshore from the Cayman Islands, you can snorkel over reefs or dive deep among coral canyons. In one shallow, sandy spot, stingrays gather to feed on fish brought by tourists. The stingrays will swim right up to snorkelers, close enough so that people can touch them with their hands. It's safe as long as no one comes in contact with the stinging spur at the base of a stingray's tail.

- La Caleta, a marine park in the Dominican Republic, contains a ship called the *Hickory*. The ship was deliberately sunk to create a site where corals could attach and create an artificial reef.

- Off the southwest corner of Puerto Rico is a coral reef that forms a wall of sorts. Scuba divers can descend along the wall and see black corals, nurse sharks, and moray eels. They may also see fish called groupers, which can weigh several hundred pounds each.

- Almost two-thirds of St. John, an island in the U.S. Virgin Islands, is designated as national park, part of Virgin Islands National Park. If you're not hiking in its green hills, you can snorkel in the 5,600 acres (2,240 hectares) of underwater park, which includes coral reef. It even has a nature trail—underwater! While snorkeling along the trail, you can read the signs placed in the sea bottom to learn about the ecology of the coral reef.

- In the Lesser Antilles, the island of Anguilla, which in Italian means "eel," is shaped a bit like one. Off this flat, dusty island is a reef with beautiful star corals, sea fans, elkhorn corals, staghorn corals, trumpet fish, damselfish, and more.

- Antigua has magnificent reefs with a variety of corals, stingrays, barracudas, parrot fish, and other animals. You can see 80 to 150 feet (24.4 to 45.7 meters) down in its clear waters to view reefs or any of the six shipwrecks close to its shores.

- St. Lucia, nestled in between the Caribbean Sea and the Atlantic Ocean, has 24 miles (38.7 kilometers) of coral reef. Some parts of the reef are not well explored because ocean currents on the Atlantic side can be strong. Coral arches, caves, canyons, and 6-foot- (1.8-meter-) tall sponges are the major attractions. Two planes were sunk near the island to provide artificial reef where corals could settle and grow.

- The Netherlands Antilles are nicknamed the ABC islands, for the first letters of their names: Aruba, Bonaire, and Curaçao. These islands lie off the coast of Venezuela. Bonaire is famous for its thousands of pink flamingos and

Sponges look like plants but are actually animals. These purple tube sponges are found off Bonaire.

for its coral reefs, which drop off into a vertical wall of coral just offshore. The entire coast of Bonaire is a marine park, home to 80 species of coral and 270 species of fish. The government has taken steps to protect the reef animals by banning spear guns used for underwater hunting, and prohibiting the dropping of boat anchors on coral reefs. The island is developing quickly with tourist resorts and facilities, which host the divers who visit from all over the world.

- Belize has the second longest barrier reef in the world, stretching almost 140 miles (225 kilometers). Its famous Lighthouse Reef Atoll is a wide ring of coral, with a dark blue center at least 400 feet (122 meters) deep. Along the barrier reef are schools of squid and angelfish, and bright orange and red corals.

The coral reefs mentioned here are only a few of the magnificent reefs of this region. Sparkling waters, sandy beaches, warm temperatures, coconut trees, and colorful reefs make parts of the Gulf of Mexico and the Caribbean seem like paradise to many.

☆ 3 ☆
CORALS:
THE REEF BUILDERS

The Great Barrier Reef can be seen by astronauts from space. Yet coral reefs are made by small, soft-bodied animals that are no bigger than a person's thumb. To understand the coral reef biome you have to know about these tiny architects, the corals: how they live and what they need to survive.

WHAT CORALS ARE

Individual corals, called polyps, are small, soft-bodied animals that sit inside hard cups made of limestone. Polyps can live together in colonies made up of hundreds, thousands, or even millions of individuals. These colonies can survive for decades, and some have been known to survive for more than a century.

A coral colony may be as tiny as a golf ball or bigger than a car. Some colonies form thin crusts; others branch out like trees. Brain corals grow in spherical mounds with rippled surfaces that make them look like human brains. Some coral species always grow in the same shapes. But others are "shape shifters" of a sort. In well-lit waters, they form rounded corals or branching corals. But in dim waters, they grow into wide, flat shelves.

The Flower Animals Corals are closely related to sea anemones—creatures that have waving tentacles and stinging cells. Both are classified as Anthozoa, a name that comes from the Greek words *anthos*, meaning "flower," and *zoon*, meaning "animal." As their name indicates, the coral animal looks a little like a flower but has tentacles instead of petals. It feeds on plankton—small, floating animals—and particles that get caught on the sticky mucus covering its tentacles. Hairlike cilia sweep the mucus and food into the coral's mouth, located in the center of its crown of tentacles. The coral's body only has one opening—the mouth—so waste products are "spit" out of this hole, too.

Polyp Particulars In general, coral polyps are tiny, no thicker than a pencil and less than 1 inch (2.5 centimeters) high. The polyps in a colony are connected by coenosarc, a thin skin of tissue that covers the limestone between them. Below each polyp's cup is a column of limestone that it has made over the years. Over time, the coral secretes more and more limestone below itself. A reef can grow at a rate of 0.3 to 1 inch (8 to 25 millimeters) per year. A brain coral may live for more than 1,000 years. But only the thin layer of living coral polyps on the reef's surface is alive; the bulk of the reef is nonliving limestone below.

This photograph shows coral with polyps closed. The inset photo shows the same coral with polyps extended.

Coral Pals   Most coral reef visitors never see a coral polyp's tentacles. That's because polyps of most corals only extend their tentacles at night to sweep the water and catch food. Additional food comes from their special plant partners, zooxanthellae. Zooxanthellae are single-celled algae that have a symbiotic relationship with coral. (A symbiotic relationship is one in which one or more partners benefits from the arrangement.) These algae, of the species *Symbiodinium microadriaticum*, live inside the coral's body tissues. Like all plants, these algae carry out photosynthesis and create food using sunlight, water, carbon dioxide, and minerals. The algae help feed the coral. They also increase the rate at which corals build their limestone skeletons. In turn, the algae receive a protected place to live.

Builders and "Decorators"   All corals secrete calcium carbonate, the chemical that makes up limestone. But not all corals make enough limestone to build large structures such as reefs. Corals that build reefs are called hermatypic corals. All these reef-building species are hard corals. Ahermatypic corals, those that do not build reefs, include soft corals, black corals, thorny corals, and horny corals. One of the reasons these corals do not secrete much calcium carbonate is that they do not have the zooxanthellae—the "partners" that help corals build reefs.

Non-reef-building corals, however, are the most colorful on the reef. They can be red, purple, orange, or pink. Their names—sea pansy, organ-pipe coral, sea fan, sea plume, sea pen—reflect their shapes, which also vary widely. These colorful corals, gently waving in the current, can make a coral reef look like an underwater flower garden.

WHAT CORALS NEED

Reef-building corals need warm seawater and plenty of light to thrive. So coral reefs are only found in the warm

A sea pen looks a lot like a feathery quill pen.

waters of the tropics and subtropics, primarily between 30° latitude north of the equator and 30° south. Even in the tropics, cold water currents can make coral reefs impossible in some spots. Cold currents make coral reefs scarce off the western coast of Africa and the western coast of the United States. Occasionally, a cold snap kills corals at the northern-most portion of their range. In January 1991, in Florida, cold temperatures dropped water temperatures to 61°F (16°C) for ten days and killed many reef corals and fish.

Sunny Shallows   To carry on photosynthesis, the algae that live inside corals need sunlight. So coral reefs develop in relatively shallow waters, 230 feet (70 meters) deep or less. Coral reefs form near continents or islands, where shallow waters exist. How deep the coral grows depends on how clear the water is and how far light can penetrate. Soft corals, which do not build reefs and do not have zooxanthellae, can live in deeper waters and colder oceans. Off the coast of Norway, soft corals form small thickets underwater. But these coral clumps are nowhere near the size and complexity of real coral reefs.

Clear and Salty   Fresh water, which is not as salty as seawater, can kill corals. So coral reefs do not form where rivers dump their fresh water into the ocean. Mud from rivers can also smother corals, which need clear water to thrive. That is one reason why coral reefs do not grow where the Amazon River pours its muddy water into the Atlantic Ocean.

SEX AND WAR AMONG CORALS

Like plants, coral polyps, once they settle down, do not travel from place to place. They settle and grow, often competing with one another for space. And they spread to new areas by reproducing.

Let's Split   Corals can build long columns of coral below them, but the animals themselves never grow very big. To expand horizontally, coral colonies must produce new polyps. They do this by dividing, literally splitting into two identical halves. Each half then grows to full size. By dividing over and over, a coral grows out, may branch, or spreads like a shelf. This is asexual reproduction because it produces polyps genetically identical to the original.

The Travelers   When a colony matures, it forms planulae—tiny young corals. Planulae are formed in two different ways. Some are formed asexually, by one colony alone. (These are genetically similar to the other polyps in that colony.) Other planulae are formed sexually. Simultaneously, all over a reef, certain corals release sperm while others release eggs. The sperm fertilize the eggs and form planulae, each of which is genetically different from its parent corals. The planulae swim upward and float through the water. A few days or weeks later, they settle and transform into polyps. During reproduction, the parent corals pass on zooxanthellae to their young. So when the planulae settle, they are fully functioning corals and can begin building their cup-like homes. That is how corals spread and establish new reefs.

Coral Wars   Corals already established on the reef battle each other for space. The combatants are different species and colonies of coral. In the laboratory, corals of different species, when placed side by side, begin a battle within a few hours. They send out long filaments, like tiny tentacles, that release chemicals to eat away parts of the other coral. The coral that is attacked may be only injured, or it may die.

Certain corals are more aggressive than others. Slow-growing corals tend to attack more quickly. Faster-growing ones rely on their quick growth to shade neighboring coral or to colonize a new place first.

REEF BUILDERS

Technically speaking, a reef is an underwater ridge, or pile, that is built upward toward the water's surface. A reef can be made of coral, rock, tires, concrete, or any other material. Oysters and mussels that grow closely packed can form a reef. Worms that cement sand together and bryozoans that form crusts of calcium can make reefs, too. But no other animal builds reefs on the size and scale that corals do.

Algae and Coral at Work   Coral reefs are built through two main processes. First, the corals—with the help of algae inside them—secrete calcium carbonate, their limestone skeletons. Second, special algae called calcareous algae do the rest of the job. (These are not the algae inside the coral tissues.) Calcareous algae cement together broken bits of coral and other sediments into solid material. They make rubble into reef, significantly stabilizing the entire coral reef.

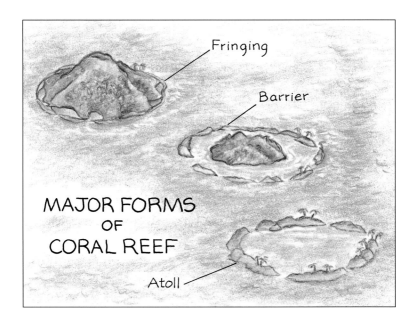

Fringe, Barrier, and Atoll   Coral reefs grow in many different forms. Three major ones are fringing reefs, barrier reefs, and atolls. Fringing reefs, as their name suggests, grow outward from the fringes of land. They are something like shelves. Atolls are rings of coral far out in the open ocean, with no land nearby. Barrier reefs form offshore, separated from the land by deep, wide lagoons. (Strangely enough, despite its name, the Great Barrier Reef isn't all barrier reef. It is a combination of many kinds.)

REEF ZONES

Coral reefs are not made up of just randomly arranged coral. Like mountains and seashores, coral reefs have zones. Each zone has different conditions. Certain kinds of animals and plants tend to be found in each of the four main coral reef zones: the lagoon, the reef flat, the reef crest, and the reef front.

Lagoon and Reef Flat   If you walked off a beach behind a coral reef, first you would reach the lagoon, which has calm waters, often with a sandy bottom. The lagoon doesn't feel the impact of ocean waves because it is protected by the reef. You might see turtle grasses, sea urchins, and flounders burying themselves in the sand. Swimming farther out, you would reach the reef flat, basically the back side of the reef. This gently sloping area has sand, mud, scattered lumps of coral, and broken coral tossed by storms. Seaweeds may grow here as well as on the reef crest, where waves break offshore.

The Reef Crest   The reef crest is the reef's highest point and receives the greatest impact of wave energy. But coral grows quickly here because the breaking waves bring in so much plankton. On some reefs, low-growing corals encrust the crest. On other reef crests, branched elkhorn corals dominate the scene. If you are snorkeling, the reef crest can be a scary place to be because coral is so close to the surface. As

Elkhorn coral looks strangely like an elk's antlers— underwater!

waves surge back and forth over the crest, they can push you against sharp branches, and you may get scraped, injuring both you and the coral reef.

Reef Front If you swim a little farther, carefully passing over the reef crest, you'll reach the reef front, also called the fore-reef. This reef section faces the open ocean, but the corals are not as close to the surface as they are on the crest, so waves do not break here. Heavy, branching corals and

Brain coral grows in mounds that have a rippled surface like a human brain.

mounds of brain coral live near the top. Deeper down, waters are calmer and wave energy is minimal; so fragile platelike corals, sea fans, and colorful soft corals thrive. The reef may plunge downward, out of sight, into deep, dim waters where black corals grow. On many islands, black coral is carved into expensive jewelry and sculptures because of its beautiful ebony shine. But in places, black coral has been overharvested for this use, so it has become quite rare.

Reef Contours Reefs have ridges, channels, caves, and holes that vary their contours, or shapes. Waves pick up coral and sediment and tumble them through the reef. This wears away gullies, creating a series of parallel ridges and canyons called a "spur and groove" formation. Water surges back and forth through these channels. Sometimes, corals grow over these grooves, forming arches and coral tunnels.

RISE AND FALL OF REEFS

The city of Chicago stands on what was once a coral reef. Its buildings are made of gravel and cement formed from the crushed shells of corals, trilobites, sea lilies, and other ancient reef creatures. Of course, back then, 410 million years ago, Chicago was ocean-covered, warm, and much nearer to the equator. As any Chicagoan shoveling snow will tell you, things have certainly changed!

Ups and Downs The earth is an ever-changing planet. Over hundreds, thousands, and millions of years, ocean levels rise and fall. The skin of the earth—the land—moves, too. Coastlines rise and sink. The sea floor pushes upward, forming volcanoes, or sinks with the weight of lava. All these ups and downs affect coral reefs drastically.

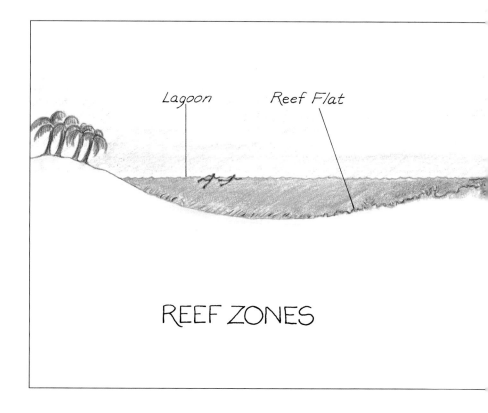

Lagoon   Reef Flat

REEF ZONES

Mystery ... Solved! In 1842, Charles Darwin, the naturalist who proposed the theory of natural selection in evolution, also came up with a startling theory about coral reefs. He believed that atolls could develop from fringing reefs surrounding volcanic islands. If a volcanic island sank, a ring of coral—an atoll—would be left behind. (The same thing happens if the sea rises, covering the volcanic island, and the coral grows upward with sea-level rise.) Almost a century later, Darwin's reef theory was proven correct. Drilling down into a coral atoll in the Pacific, scientists found the cone of a sunken volcano below. Today, scientists also believe that barrier reefs form from fringing reefs as the land sinks or the water level rises.

Reef Crest

Reef Front

History Reefs have come and gone in various periods of the earth's history. At times, the earth's climate has been too cold for reefs to survive. And the reef builders have not always been corals; bryozoans—mosslike marine animals— built reefs 500 million years ago. But for the last ten thousand years, since the last ice age, coral reefs have existed in a relatively stable environment. Animals and plants have adapted to these conditions, creating a rich and colorful biome.

✫ 4 ✫
CORAL REEF RESIDENTS

With snorkel-like snouts, inflatable bodies, poisonous spines, and detachable arms, reef creatures have an array of adaptations worthy of superheroes and cartoon worlds. There are flounders that change colors to match their backgrounds. Anemones wave stinging tentacles, like made-up monsters in a film. Fish are "dressed" in Day-Glo colors, with stripes, spots, and false eyes on their tails. And some coral reef residents form relationships that are almost too strange to believe.

WHO'S WHO ON THE REEF

Coral reefs have one of the widest assortments of animals and plants anywhere on earth. Most reef-dwelling plants are algae. Zooxanthellae live inside corals. Others grow on the surface of the reef. What people commonly call "seaweeds" are actually large forms of algae. Reefs also have phytoplankton—tiny, often microscopic plants, including algae, that float in the water surrounding the reef. Together, these plants form the basis of the coral reef community.

Spineless Ones Coral reefs are a haven for invertebrates—animals without backbones. Reef invertebrates include corals, jellyfish, seahorses, sponges, sea anemones, worms, sea stars, sea urchins, eels, crabs, lobsters, sea slugs, and more. These animals get along just fine without internal backbones. For example, lobsters, shrimp, and crabs have an exoskeleton, a hard, outer shell. Mollusks such as clams, snails, scallops, and conchs, have an even harder, more rigid shell to protect their soft bodies. For defense, sea stars have spiny skin with interlocking plates. Liquid-filled tubes built into their bodies act as a special kind of skeleton, called a hydrostatic skeleton. To stiffen and relax parts of their bodies, they adjust the pressure inside the tubes.

Backbone Brigade   Sea turtles, seabirds, and dolphins are regularly seen around reefs. But the main coral reef vertebrates—animals with backbones—are fishes. More fish species live on coral reefs than in other biomes. Almost 40 percent of the earth's 21,000 fish species spend time on coral reefs. A single coral reef in the Pacific Ocean may be home to 1,000 or more fish species.

The typical reef fish is not shaped like the cylindrical trout found in streams. Most reef fish have bodies that are laterally compressed. (That's a scientific way of saying it looks like someone put a hand on either side of them and squashed their bodies until they were flattened.) This shape gives fish such as tangs, angelfish, and butterfly fish good maneuverability. But not all reef fish fit this mold. Barracuda are long and thick. Puffers are rather boxy-looking until they puff up with water. Then they look more like cantaloupes with spines!

Few predators could stomach a puffer fish!

CORAL REEF DINERS

Who cares what a parrot fish eats for dinner? Tourists in the Caribbean should. The white or pink sand that tourists lounge on is a by-product of parrot fishes' meals. Parrot fish bite coral off the reef. Then they chew it up to get the algae that live inside. The leftovers—a fine, pink or white coral sand—are deposited as parrot fish droppings. One adult parrot fish can produce an estimated ton of sand each year!

Fortunately, not all reef dwellers eat coral, or there wouldn't be very much coral left. Coral reef residents have a wide range of eating habits. They also have some amazing ways to avoid becoming some other animal's meal!

· A SUBJECT THAT'S FULL OF HOLES ·

The sponges you see in your bathroom or kitchen are probably made of plastic. But before plastic sponges, people used the dead remains of real sponges—a type of animal—for the same purpose. Some people still use real sponges today, but they are more expensive than the plastic ones.

Sponges are animals that belong to the phylum Porifera, meaning "bearing pores." There are about 5,000 species, mostly marine, although a few live in freshwater habitats. As adults, sponges are sessile, meaning they stay in one place. As water flows through the holes in their bodies, sponges filter out particles of food. Only the larvae of sponges travel. The larvae float through the water, spreading to new places; then they settle down, attach to a surface, and grow into adults.

Sponges can be smaller than a marble or larger than a refrigerator. They can be colorful, not just brown but bright red, yellow, orange, green, or purple. Like corals, sponges grow in many shapes: some branch, others are round, some coat rocks

---

Nibblers, Scrapers, and Grazers Many coral reef animals—including sea urchins, sea slugs, cowries, bristleworms, butterfly fish, puffers, and triggerfish—nibble on coral polyps or eat algae they scrape off the reef. Damselfish tend lawns of stringy algae that grow on the reef. They graze on the algae for food. They keep away other grazers and bite off corals that try to grow on their algae lawn.

Stomach It The most famous coral eaters are the crown-of-thorns sea stars, relatives of starfish, which live in the Indian and Pacific Oceans. Their thorny name comes from the poisonous spines that cover them. To eat coral, a crown-

in a thin layer. Some look like vases, fingers, or fans. Others bore holes into mollusks or rocks, which they dissolve and absorb for minerals.

Sponges are ancient animals, among the simplest multicellular animals on earth. They have no real organs, such as lungs or a heart. Their bodies are made of a gelatinous material stiffened by spicules—tiny pieces of silica or calcium. Not all sponges are as spongy as a bath sponge; many are much stiffer. Water flows into sponges through tiny holes called ostia, and flows out through larger holes called oscula. The water flows through the sponges in canals where hairlike flagella sweep the water along.

Sponges play an important role on coral reefs. They are home to crabs, nudibranchs, fishes, and other animals that hide within their pores. Turtles, fishes, and mollusks eat some species of sponges. *Dromia* crabs put sponges on their backs to use as camouflage! Without sponges, the coral reef would be a very different habitat indeed. So next time you see a household sponge, think of its origins—those amazing living sponges of the sea.

Tube feet are clearly visible on the underside of this crown-of-thorns sea star.

of-thorns sea star turns its stomach inside out and pushes it through its mouth. The stomach covers the coral polyps and digests them with chemicals. In one day, an adult sea star can eat 2 square feet (0.18 square meter) of coral. Periodically, the population of these sea stars drastically increases. More sea stars eat more corals, damaging reefs.

Crowns of thorns are so damaging to corals that some other animals that also feed on corals try to get rid of them. To defend their coral home, *Trapezia* crabs will grab a crown of thorns and shake it until it moves away. Pistol shrimp rush at the sea stars, snapping their claws noisily. They'll even nudge the sea stars and snap their claws some more. Crowns of thorns usually avoid the coral species that are defended by these crabs or shrimp.

Soup's On   Coral reefs are bathed in a soup of food particles. Most particles are so small you would not even notice

34

· WHALE, FISH, OR SHARK? ·

Whales and fish may look somewhat alike, but they are actually very different. Whales and dolphins are mammals and need to breathe air. Fish can get oxygen from water by filtering it through their gills. Marine mammals, such as whales, dolphins, and seals, give birth to live young. They feed their babies milk. Some fish lay eggs; others bear live young. But they do not feed their babies milk.

Sharks are fish—a special kind of fish. Most of their skeleton is made of cartilage, not bone. Cartilage is a little bit softer and more flexible than bone. Sharks, along with their relatives—skates and rays—are collectively called elasmobranchs. Elasmobranchs all have bodies containing mostly cartilage instead of bones. Most other reef fish are bony fish. They have hard bones, not just cartilage.

---

them. But many animals, including corals, dine on this nutritious food. What's in the soup? Plankton is one ingredient. Animal droppings are in there, too. Leftover morsels from others' meals and bits of decaying animals and plants add to the broth.

The "soup drinkers" are called suspension feeders because they eat foods suspended in the water. Clams pull in water through siphons—which are something like hoses—and filter out the food. Sponges pump water through their porous bodies to capture tiny bits of food. Sea anemones catch food particles on their sticky, mucus-covered tentacles. Christmas tree worms and feather duster worms filter food from the water flowing by. Their names come from the feathery gills they use to snare food particles.

Predator Parade   How do you eat a spiny sea urchin? Triggerfish blow a stream of water at an urchin until they knock it over. Then they dine on its soft underside. The triggerfish's trick is one of many techniques predators use to capture prey. Barracuda, which patrol the waters above the reef, have long bodies built for quick bursts of speed and sharp teeth to grab prey fish once they've caught up with them. Corals, sea anemones, and jellyfish have stinging cells called cnidocytes. These cells shoot out barbs that penetrate the prey animal's flesh. The barbs release toxins that can sting, paralyze, or kill an animal, depending on its size. These cells are used in catching food but may also be used in defense.

Defensive Lines   With so many coral reef predators on the prowl, prey animals need good defenses. One technique is to avoid detection. Fish have colors, shapes, and patterns that blend in with the reef. To mask their bodies' smell, parrot fish sleep in bags of mucus, so predators, mainly moray eels, will have a harder time finding them. Once discovered, many animals use secondary lines of defense to discourage predators. Sea urchins' spines, for instance, can keep away most hungry mouths, although not the triggerfish's. (Sea urchin spines can also pierce a careless scuba diver's finger, boot, or fin.) When threatened, puffers fill themselves with water so that they look too big to eat and their poisonous spines stick out. Nudibranchs—sea slugs—get their defenses from the food they eat. They eat hydroids, relatives of sea anemones and jellyfish. Hydroids are covered with stinging cells. Strangely, the cells don't harm the sea slug. The sea slug is able to distribute the stinging cells throughout its body, helping it to defend itself.

Escape Artists   A popular defense is a quick escape. A fish may dive into a crevice to hide. Other animals have tricks to

· JELLYFISH ADVICE ·

If you see Australian swimmers wearing panty hose, don't be shocked by their fashion mistake. Near Australia's Great Barrier Reef, dangerous jellyfish are common. So, some swimmers wear panty hose to protect their legs from stings! Fortunately, most jellyfish are much less dangerous, causing only itchy rashes that last for several hours.

Portuguese man-of-war

The stings of the lion's mane jellyfish and the Portuguese man-of-war can be deadly, though. Your legs may cramp, you may have trouble breathing and swimming, you may even die without medical attention. Lion's mane jellyfish and Portuguese man-of-wars aren't common along most U.S. beaches. But Portuguese man-of-wars are found in Florida and other tropical waters near coral reefs. Here is some advice on dealing with jellyfish you may encounter:

- Don't touch jellyfish, even dead ones. Their stinging cells can still be activated when the animals are dead.
- If you get a jellyfish sting on your skin, sprinkle meat tenderizer on it as soon as possible. The enzymes in the meat tenderizer break down the jellyfish stingers still in the skin. This helps relieve itching and pain.
- Consult a doctor immediately for serious symptoms such as difficulty breathing. People who get several jellyfish stings, or even just one sting from a lion's mane jellyfish or a Portuguese man-of-war, will need to see a doctor.

confuse predators. Like a magician who disappears in a cloud of smoke, an octopus will squirt out a cloud of ink to hide itself and then quickly swim away. To escape an attacker, a crab will abandon a claw, and a sea star will abandon an arm. Luckily, these animals can regenerate new parts, although it does take energy and time.

COLOR AND CAMOUFLAGE

Most of the ocean is murky, dimly lit, or out of sunlight's reach. But coral reefs occur in shallow, clear water where colors can easily be seen. As a result, coral reefs are the most colorful ocean habitats on earth. What these colors mean and how they benefit animals is often a puzzle to scientists.

Advertise! One way animals use color is to advertise. Males or females may have bright colors to attract mates. Some fish species have brighter colors or special patterns during mating season, for instance. The tiny blue-ringed octopus is colorful for another reason entirely. This plum-sized octopus is more poisonous than any rattlesnake. Its colors warn predators to stay away.

Colorful Conversations Color is also used to communicate moment to moment. Fish called Moorish idols turn brighter colors when they fight. Squid, octopi, and cuttlefish are the masters of colorful conversation. Squid can change their skin color to pink, red, purple, gray, or speckled combinations of many colors within seconds.

These colors communicate a squid's mood—whether it's surprised, ready to fight, ready to mate, and so on. The squid controls its colors using chromatophores—tiny sacs of colored pigment in its skin. When a sac is spread out, that color shows; when it's squeezed tight, that color is less noticeable.

Wearing Camo Unless you are a poisonous, dangerous animal, colorful advertising can be dangerous. The showier you are, the better chance predators will find you. So, many fish are camouflaged, meaning they have colors, markings, and shapes that help hide them in their habitat. Camouflage can be brightly colored. Near a yellow coral, for instance, a bright yellow fish may blend in perfectly. Many reef fish have bold stripes and blotches that break up their outlines so that predators will not recognize their shapes. Stripes through the eye help conceal the eye, an otherwise vulnerable, easily recognized spot. A few reef fish have fake eyespots on their bodies or fins. A predator may lunge for these fake features and miss the more essential parts, lessening the injury to the prey animal. Or, the predator may be confused about whether the animal is coming or going, and which way the animal will retreat.

Camouflage isn't just for hiding from predators; it's also for hunting stealthily. Batfish and flounder match the sand and mud where they settle and wait for prey. Frogfish are orange, yellow, or pink, depending on the color of the coral where they live. When an unsuspecting fish passes by, these sit-and-wait predators rise up and grab their meal. Animals that are not born camouflaged may acquire it later.

Decorator crabs cover themselves with algae and sponges to hide on the reef.

Marine Mimics If you see an animal with dots, an eye-spot, and a curved form, sticking out of a crevice in a reef, you may have found a spotted moray eel. Or, it could be a marine betta—a type of fish. Bettas mimic spotted moray eels. The betta hides headfirst in a crevice, sticking out its spotted, rounded tail, which has a spot that looks like an eel's eye. Another mimic is the shrimpfish, which is slender and black-striped. It hides by hovering, head-down, among a sea urchin's spines. Trumpet fish, on the other hand, use mimicry to help in hunting. Long and slender-bodied, they hide among the branches of a finger sponge. Then, when a small fish passes by the sponge, the trumpet fish simply snaps up the fish in its long snout.

Not Like Dad Black with yellow stripes, a young gray angelfish looks very little like its solid gray parents. Such differences are common in reef fish. In some cases, though, the young fish have colors that conceal them from predators. The adults' colors are bolder, presumably for displays to defend territories and attract mates.

STRANGE RELATIONSHIPS

Over thousands of years, coral reef animals have evolved symbiotic relationships—relationships in which at least one of them benefits. Indeed, reefs would not exist without the symbiotic relationship between corals and zooxanthellae—the algae that live inside them and help build reefs.

Types of Partnerships There are three main types of symbiotic relationship. One is parasitism: a relationship in which one animal benefits and the other one suffers a loss.

A second type is commensalism: a relationship in which one animal benefits and the other one does not benefit, but is not damaged either. A third type is mutualism: a relationship in which both partners benefit. (Many nonscientists use the term *symbiosis* to mean this kind of relationship. But scientists like to be more specific and use the term *mutualism* instead.) Although all three types of symbiosis occur in biomes worldwide, some of the best-known examples are found in coral reefs.

Fish Dentists and Cleaners   Twisting its body and undulating its fins, a tiny, brightly colored fish called a wrasse advertises its occupation: cleaner fish. Bigger fish line up at "cleaning stations" to have their teeth, skin, gills, and mouths picked clean of large parasites by the wrasse. The cleaner fish even cleans wounds of dead skin and debris, making wounds heal faster than they would on their own. This is a classic mutualistic relationship. The wrasse gets a meal; the big fish gets clean. The big fish won't eat the little wrasse, even when it swims inside its mouth. Wrasses aren't the only cleaners. Gobies, butterfly fish, and immature gray angelfish clean fish, too. And banded coral shrimp set up cleaning stations where they clean moray eels.

In recent years, scientists have discovered the cleaner fish relationship is even more complex than they once thought. It turns out that cleaner fish remove some healthy scales and bits of fin, along with parasites and dead flesh. So they're not entirely helpful, after all. Scientists suspect the big fish put up with the cleaning not just because it's beneficial, but because it's pleasurable, like having an itch scratched. How important are cleaner fish? Studies show that when they are removed from a reef, many of the other fish leave.

Another fish, however, is a parasite in disguise. The

saber-toothed blenny looks like a cleaner fish and uses that to its advantage. As the big fish holds still, waiting to be cleaned, the blenny darts in close. It takes a bite of the big fish and quickly swims away!

Home Security   It is difficult to pry a sea anemone off a reef. But some species of hermit crab have just the right touch. They pick up small sea anemones and carefully place them on their own shells. The hermit crab gets a protective armor—the anemones' stinging tentacles—plus it's good camouflage. Scientists are not sure how the sea anemones benefit from the ride on the hermit crab; perhaps the anemones get scraps that float up when the hermit crab feeds. But scientists do know it's a long-term partnership. When the hermit crab grows too big for its old shell, it moves into a new one. It carefully transfers the anemones from its old shell to the new.

Clown Fish and Anemones   Clown fish are small, colorful fish that spend most of their lives near anemones. They hover in between the anemones' tentacles, yet somehow never get stung. Clown fish have a special coating of mucus that seems to protect them from the stings. Clown fish help the anemones by chasing off butterfly fish, which often dine on anemones. The anemones may get morsels from the fish's meals. But the clown fish also benefit, because they can hide out in the anemones' stinging tentacles, where other predators will not pursue them.

The Guard Dog Goby   Pistol shrimp dig burrows in the sand in and around coral reefs. Each one of these near-sighted shrimp shares its burrow with a fish called a goby. The goby and the pistol shrimp spend most of their time foraging for food outside, near the burrow entrance. When

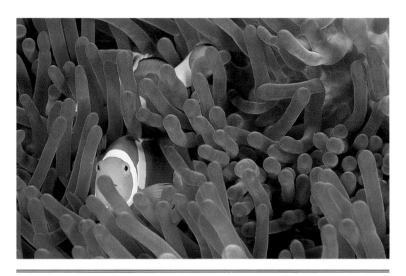

*An anemone's stinging tentacles
don't bother these clown fish a bit.*

a predator approaches, the goby flicks its tail, touching the shrimp's antenna to alert it. Both of them then retreat to the safety of the burrow. It's an arrangement that works well for both. The goby gets a place to hide—in the shrimp's burrow. In turn, the shrimp gets a built-in alarm.

Hiders and Hitchhikers   Some small fish use sponges as hideouts, darting inside when danger approaches. Others, thin and striped, dart in among sea urchin spines to hide. These are both cases of commensalism, because one partner benefits, with little harm to the other. Another commensal relationship is between remoras—a kind of fish—and reef visitors such as turtles, sharks, and manta rays. The remora has a suction disk on its underside, which it uses to stick to turtles, sharks, and manta rays, even when these animals swim at high speed. The remora isn't along for the ride. When its host feeds, the remora comes loose and feeds on

Parrot fish have strong front teeth that resemble a parrot's beak.

scraps. Then it sticks back on and travels with its host, who is not harmed.

NIGHT AND DAY ON THE CORAL REEF

As evening approaches, a sort of "changing of the guard" occurs on coral reefs. Parrot fish, angelfish, and snappers, which are active during the day, settle down low on the reef and hide under overhangs. At the same time, night creatures emerge from crevices where they have been hiding all day. Squirrelfish, which have large eyes for better light reception, swim higher in the water and begin to feed. Moray eels undulate out of their hiding spots. Octopi start to swim. Lobsters and shrimp crawl out of their holes and begin to scavenge food on the reef. Corals extend their tentacles and worms push out their feathery gills to gather food particles from water passing by. These night animals dominate the coral reef until morning, when the day creatures take over once again.

☆ 5 ☆
CORAL REEF COMMUNITIES

In the ocean, animals and plants are not distributed evenly, like grass on a well-kept lawn. Animals and plants clump together in certain places, while much of the rest of the ocean is relatively bare. Coral reefs are one of the places where marine animals and plants cluster. They are extremely productive habitats, producing large amounts of food. Coral reefs also have existed for thousands of years, and this has allowed a great diversity of coral reef species to evolve.

DAZZLING DIVERSITY

Coral reefs have an extremely high animal diversity. Nowhere else in the ocean can you find so many kinds of fish and invertebrates. A Pacific coral reef may contain up to 3,000 species of organisms. A Caribbean reef can contain 1,000 or more. Because of their diversity, coral reefs are often called the tropical rain forests of the ocean. That's because tropical rain forests have the highest diversity of animal and plant species of any biome on earth.

Fabulous Phyla   Tropical rain forests have more species—kinds of animals and plants—than coral reefs. But coral reefs have animals that belong to more phyla—major

It's easy to see how feather duster worms got their name!

animal groups. Scientists divide animals into thirty-three major phyla according to their characteristics. Animals of thirty-two phyla are found in the ocean, whereas only seventeen phyla live on land. Some of the phyla live both in the ocean and on land. From jellyfish to crabs to manta rays to feather duster worms, you cannot beat a coral reef for sheer variety of body types of animals.

Living Together   The many animal species on coral reefs could not live together long if they tried to eat the same food, at the same time, in the same way. Eventually, they would compete with each other. Some would "lose" the competition and die off. On a coral reef, thousands of species can live together because each has its own way of life. Among fish, for example, some eat algae, some eat other fish, some swim high in the water, some swim low in the water, some feed at night, and some feed during the day. Each has its own niche—its own role in the coral reef community. And these animals are interdependent—they depend on one another in many different ways.

AMAZING FOOD FACTORY

On coral reefs, the main organisms that create food for themselves are algae: zooxanthellae living inside corals, calcareous algae that cement corals together, green mats of algae that encrust corals, and phytoplankton in the surrounding waters. Almost every other coral reef organism depends on these plants, directly or indirectly, for food. If an organism does not eat algae, it either eats something that eats algae or the leftovers and by-products of eating algae.

Be Productive! A farmer calls a farm productive if the fields yield plenty of corn and wheat. A rancher calls a field productive if the cows eating the grass grow fat. Ecologists try to measure the same kinds of productivity for natural habitats. They measure the weight of a sampling of the plant and animal material that is produced by the biome each year. Overall, coral reefs are considered very productive, especially when compared to the unproductive ocean waters nearby.

Awesome Oasis The tropical waters where coral reefs grow are beautifully clear precisely because they are so poor in nutrients. (Water in more productive parts of the ocean can be murky because it is so full of living animals and plants.) For scientists, finding coral reefs in these waters is like finding an oasis of green trees in the midst of a lifeless desert. Scientists are still a little puzzled by how coral reefs can be so productive under these conditions. They do know that one key to a coral reef's productivity is recycling. Not

· DIVE IN! ·

Seeing a coral reef firsthand is one of the most amazing experiences you can have. You can watch turtles swim, squid dart, and fish feed. The three main ways of visiting a coral reef are snorkeling, scuba diving, and in glass-bottom boats.

Snorkeling

Snorkeling, also called skin diving, is easy to learn and inexpensive to do. You wear a clear mask on your face so that you can see the reef. You breathe through a snorkel—a long, J-shaped plastic tube. One end of the tube goes in your mouth. The other end sticks out of the water. Many people also wear plastic or rubber flippers on their feet to make their swimming kick more powerful. Snorkeling is easy, once you get the hang of it. It can be done by almost anyone, young or old. You swim quietly along the water's surface, looking down through the mask at the reef and breathing through the tube. To get a closer look at the reef, you can hold your breath and dive down. When you come up, you blow out hard to clear your snorkel of water, then breathe again. To learn how to snorkel, it's best to practice first in a swimming pool so that you will be comfortable when you get

much goes to waste. You won't see a pileup of leftover food or dead animals in a coral reef. There are animals that quickly snap these up. Plentiful sunlight, warm temperatures, and plenty of surface area for plants to grow also help make coral reefs productive.

to a coral reef. For snorkeling classes, check your local pool, dive shop, YMCA, YWCA, community college, or university.

SCUBA stands for Self-Contained Underwater Breathing Apparatus. Scuba diving takes more training than snorkeling and it can be quite a bit more expensive because you need to rent tanks and gear. With scuba, however, you carry tanks of air on your back, so you can dive deeply without holding your breath. Scuba allows you to swim underwater for an hour or more. You can really see the reef animals up close. To scuba dive, you need to take classes and become certified. These classes are held in swimming pools. In scuba classes you will learn both how to snorkel and scuba dive. To take the class you usually need a physician's permission and you need to be able to swim. Scuba diving can be dangerous, even deadly, if done improperly. Good training is essential. For classes, contact your local scuba diving shop, community college, or university.

You can see a coral reef without even getting wet. Some tourist companies near coral reefs run glass-bottom boats and small submarines. You can ride in these vehicles and look through the windows at the coral reef.

If you cannot visit a coral reef, visit an aquarium instead! Many aquariums in major cities have gigantic tanks with fish, shrimp, lobsters, corals, sharks, sea turtles, and even stingrays. Just be sure to set aside plenty of time for your visit. You'll be amazed at what you'll find.

Sister Habitats   Most coral reef communities depend on two other important habitats: sea grass beds and mangrove swamps. Sea grass beds are underwater lawns of sea grass, where turtles, young fish, crabs, and mollusks feed. Many animals spend part of the day or part of their lives in the sea grass beds and the other part in coral reefs. Sea grass beds also filter the water and stabilize the sand and mud near coral reefs.

Mangrove swamps are semiaquatic wetlands that grow on tropical shores. Mangrove trees grow partly in and partly out of the water. Underwater, mangrove trees' arching roots form a perfect place for young fishes to hide. Mangroves act as a nursery, where many juvenile reef-dwelling animals grow up, before moving out to the reef. Mangroves are also important because their roots trap sediment, stabilizing shorelines. And they filter out pollutants that run off the land, preventing pollution from reaching coral reefs. For all these reasons and many more, healthy mangrove swamps and sea grass beds are essential to the survival of coral reefs. Scientists consider all three habitats to be part of an overall coral reef ecosystem.

FRAGILE YET RESILIENT

A coral reef can live for thousands of years. Yet, in one day, a hurricane can flatten it. Strong waves and currents can topple fragile corals and sweep the ocean bottom clean. Other natural forces can destroy coral reefs, too. Water that is too warm, too cold, too muddy, or not salty enough can kill corals. Even sea stars can eat large portions of the living coral on the reef. Nevertheless, coral reefs survive and re-grow even after these natural disasters. It just takes time, of course, and reefs must be healthy to begin with, to recover properly.

Hurricanes   Hurricanes are undoubtedly the greatest natural destroyers of coral reefs. These massive storms can have winds of more than 200 miles (323 kilometers) per hour. The winds whip up waves that destroy the reefs. In August 1980, Hurricane Allen hit Jamaica's Discovery Bay reefs, which had been almost untouched for more than thirty years. Eight years later, Hurricane Gilbert hit, and the next year, Hurricane Hugo. The coral reefs were effectively scoured away. Scientists estimate that some parts of the reef will take a few decades to recover, while others may take a century.

Other Physical Events   Physical events other than hurricanes can damage coral reefs. In the tropics, weather conditions are usually fairly stable throughout the year. But, at times, unusually cold or warm weather can occur, killing corals over large areas. (Usually these die-offs happen on the edges of the coral reef range, where corals are living in conditions very close to the minimum they need.) Heavy rains can also kill corals, by drenching them with fresh water and lowering the water's salinity. Heavy rains can also swell rivers on land, causing them to carry loads of mud and sand to the ocean, where they smother coral reefs. Unusually low tides can also kill corals because they expose the reefs to the drying air. The ultraviolet rays of the sun can kill corals if the water is unusually calm or clear and more light than normal is reaching the corals below.

Attack of the Hungry Mouths   Strangely enough, even hungry organisms can eat away the living skin of the coral reef. In large numbers, coral-eating animals such as sea stars, sea urchins, puffers, snails, and worms can seriously damage a reef. Diseases such as black band disease damage corals as well. Black band disease begins as a small spot on coral, but in a few months it can expand, killing an entire coral colony. The leading edges of the disease form a black band, hence its name. In the last ten years, newly discovered diseases such as yellow band, white band, and purple band have been killing corals as well.

*This brain coral shows the damage
caused by black band disease.*

· THE CROWN-OF-THORNS SEA STAR ·

Crown-of-thorns sea stars, which occur in the Pacific and Indian Oceans, can literally eat a reef's living coral, scouring its surface clean. These prickly predators can grow to 1 foot (30 centimeters) or more in diameter, about the size of a Frisbee. For unknown reasons, the populations of these sea stars increase drastically some years. When one sea star eats, it releases a chemical that attracts others of its kind. So they gather in great numbers, eating up large parts of reefs such as the Great Barrier Reef. It may take twenty years or more for the reefs they attack to recover. In the Maldive Islands, scuba divers are asked to pry sea stars off the reef to help control their populations. At one resort, they removed over 18,000 in a year!

Recovery Coral reefs can recover after some seemingly disastrous events. After a hurricane, dead fish and invertebrates float in the water and wash up on beaches. But within a few years, most animal populations can recover, given the chance. For example, in the Caribbean, several hurricanes occur each year, but a given reef is hit only once every seven years, on average. Coral reefs, in a limited way, are adapted to such events. Elkhorn coral branches that break off can regenerate into new colonies. The storms may even help some coral species spread. Floating larvae from other corals settle in spaces left by dead ones. These larvae grow new colonies.

THE MYSTERY OF THE DYING REEFS

In the winter of 1982–1983, half the coral reefs on the Pacific side of Costa Rica died. In the Galápagos, most of the corals died, too. Reefs, which the year before had been colorful with corals and sponges, were suddenly, startlingly white. As the years went on, through the 1980s and early 1990s, coral reefs near Florida, Puerto Rico, Jamaica, Grand Cayman, Australia, Japan, Oman, Indonesia, Hawaii, Bermuda, and other locales turned white as well. These reefs were undergoing a global, reef-threatening phenomenon called coral bleaching.

Losing Their Partners Coral bleaching occurs when corals eject the colorful algae that live inside them. The leftover coral is white, so scientists call it "bleached." Bleached coral can live for a while without its algae. However, it will not grow as quickly. If it can absorb new algae soon, it may recover. But long periods of bleaching or repeated bleachings can cause the coral to die.

Hot Seas Scientists suspect that the bleaching of coral in most parts of the world is due to increases in ocean water

The bleached area in the center of this staghorn coral indicates that it is dying.

temperatures. If the sea temperature rises only 1.8 to 3.6°F (1 to 2°C) above normal for days, weeks, or months, corals can bleach and die. Most bleaching episodes have occurred at the same time scientists have recorded unusually warm temperatures in the areas where bleaching occurred. But scientists are still gathering information about bleaching and cannot prove conclusively that warm water is the cause.

Other Explanations Warm temperatures have not occurred in all the areas that bleached. Scientists are not sure what caused bleaching in cooler areas. But some suspect that the unusually calm, clear seas may have allowed too much sunlight to reach the corals. Too much ultraviolet radiation can not only sunburn people and give them skin cancer, but it apparently damages coral, too!

Wacky Weather Many bleaching episodes in warm waters were during years when El Niño, a set of disruptive weather patterns, was in force. During El Niño years, winds in the Pacific Ocean change direction. They blow warm currents of water where normally there are cold currents. In 1982–1983, El Niño caused sea temperatures to rise 9°F (5°C) in places, probably causing the deaths of the reefs in

· OZONE CONCERNS ·

These days, the earth's ozone layer—a layer of gases that shields the earth from much of the sun's ultraviolet radiation—is thinning. Chlorofluorocarbons (CFCs)—chemicals once widely used in aerosols, air-conditioning, and the manufacture of plastics—cause chemical reactions that destroy ozone. So far, the greatest thinning has occurred near the North and South Poles. But if the ozone layer over the tropics thins, coral reefs would be in great danger. Corals and other marine life are easily damaged or killed by ultraviolet rays. So far, no linkage has been found between ozone thinning and bleaching episodes.

In 1987, most countries worldwide agreed to the Montreal Protocol, which mandated a phaseout of CFCs. But the treaty does allow some production of various ozone-destroying chemicals, and environmentalists are concerned the treaty may not be enough. Even if ozone-destroying chemicals were banned today, the pollutants already released would still be traveling up into the atmosphere. It may be many years before we see the effects of those pollutants.

the Galápagos and off Costa Rica. El Niño also has widespread affects on weather around the globe.

Global Change Many people are concerned that there may be an underlying reason for the warm ocean temperatures. Most scientists agree that the earth's climate is changing, becoming warmer overall. They believe this change, all or in part, is because of air pollutants released by automobiles, industry, backyard grills, lawn mowers, and the burning of tropical forests. So far, however, the way this global change would affect oceans is unknown. An overall heating of the earth's atmosphere would not be felt evenly around the globe. It is more likely to cause shifts in the normal weather patterns, making some areas warmer, colder, rainier, or drier than they are today. As of yet, scientists do not know enough to predict what will happen to coral reefs, if the earth's climate becomes warmer.

STRIKING A BALANCE

A coral reef is a place of balance, between fishes, seaweeds, corals, and all the other reef inhabitants. Small disturbances are natural. A parrot fish may eat away a patch of coral. A few seaweeds may settle and grow in the empty space. Corals may spread out and fill in the space that is left. This kind of fluctuation is natural, like when a tree falls in a forest and lets in light so that small trees and shrubs can thrive.

Sometimes, however, coral reefs undergo much bigger, more noticeable changes. A hurricane hits. Or, suddenly, the reef is covered by algae instead of coral. Are these changes natural, useful, and helpful in the long run? Or do they doom the coral reef community? Often it is hard to know.

Some scientists believe a certain amount of stress keeps a coral reef healthy, by shifting the balance of animals on the reef. Even hurricanes, if they are not too frequent or too devastating, may be a normal part of a coral reef's life. What scientists and environmentalists are more concerned about are long-term changes that signify real trouble for coral reefs. A coral reef that could regrow after a hurricane or disease might not be able to do so if it is weakened by other factors: disease, pollution, unusually warm waters, intense ultraviolet radiation, or other stresses. A much better understanding of coral reefs is needed to predict how they will change in the years to come.

☆ 6 ☆
PEOPLE AND CORAL REEFS

In ancient Hawaii, warriors poisoned the tips of their spears with chemicals from a coral called *limu make-o-Hana*, meaning "deadly seaweed of Hana." Only one tide pool on the entire island of Maui contained the precious coral. Fortunately, the Hawaiians preserved the tide pool where the corals live, because today a derivative of that poison is used in fighting cancer.

Like that tide pool on Maui, coral reefs contain many animals that produce potentially useful chemicals. Scientists are developing anti-asthma drugs from chemicals in sea fans, painkillers from chemicals in sea whips, and anti-cancer drugs modeled after compounds in sponges. Coral reefs have great promise as a source of medicines and other products, too. This potential is just one of the many reasons why people want to protect coral reefs from the environmental problems that threaten them.

THREATS TO CORAL REEFS

In the last ten years, many scuba divers and snorkelers have visited their favorite coral reefs, only to find that much of the coral is dead. Instead of colorful corals, schools of fish, feather duster worms, and waving sea fans, they have found white, dead rubble; only a few fish species; and little else. In places, patches of coral are missing or dying because of disease. Some coral reef communities seem "out of balance." Inhabitants such as sharks, conchs, groupers, triggerfish, and lobsters are absent from where they should be. Other species such as sea urchins and algaes are too widespread.

Like any biome, coral reefs can change over time, as discussed in chapter 5. But the widespread changes divers are seeing signal serious trouble for many coral reefs. Reefs in the Philippines are among the most damaged in the world; about 90 percent have already been damaged seriously. Other reefs in the Indo-Pacific and Caribbean regions are showing signs of trouble, too. Pollution, habitat destruction, overfishing, the pet trade, and other human activities are damaging coral reefs. As described in chapter 5, natural and human-caused changes in the global climate may be affecting coral reefs as well.

Destructive Construction   When tourists flock to a certain location, such as an island or coast near coral reefs, a building boom occurs. Hotels, airports, shops, restaurants, and paved roads pop up, seemingly overnight. Not all the construction is for tourist facilities. In some areas, native populations are increasing rapidly as well, the same way human populations are increasing all over the world. And people are moving from inland to coastal cities near coral reefs. To construct buildings and roads in these areas, people often use the only plentiful building material around—coral. Countless reefs and areas around reefs are dredged for material to produce the concrete and gravel for roads and buildings.

Construction has other damaging effects on coral reefs. Land is usually cleared of trees and other plants, leaving the soil bare and vulnerable to erosion. When heavy rains come, they wash soil off the bare land into rivers or directly into the ocean. This mud and sand smothers coral reefs. Construction can also pollute coastal waters with mud, paint, solvents, and other materials used in the construction process.

Slimy Problems The more people there are, the more sewage there is. And sewage damages coral reefs. Coral reefs are adapted to grow in water that is low in nutrients. Sewage fertilizes the reef, causing an overgrowth of algae, which can outcompete corals and kill them off. Sewage also contains many harsh chemicals, heavy metals, and other toxins from products people pour down their drains or chemicals industries use. These toxins can poison reef animals.

Trash Troubles Like so many other ocean environments, coral reefs are plagued by trash. Discarded fishing lines, plastic bags, bottles, and cans show up on the reefs. Reef animals can become entangled in such trash and die. Sea turtles, who frequent reefs, often swallow plastic bags. They probably mistake them for jellyfish—a favorite turtle food. Trash such as batteries, oil cans, bug sprays, and household cleaners can leak dangerous chemicals as well. Even remote Pacific islands have trash on their shores; it is carried there by ocean currents from thousands of miles away. Trash on coral reefs comes from garbage dumped at sea, trash thrown overboard by boaters, and trash left by beachgoers. Large cruise ships, in particular, have been cited for disposing of their trash by simply throwing it overboard.

Awful Anchors At many popular diving sites, coral reefs are being damaged by divers. Diving, fishing, and snorkeling boats anchor on coral reefs so that they can stop, allowing passengers to swim and dive. When the anchors are put

Permanent moorings, installed by groups like Reef Relief, can save reefs from the damage boat anchors cause.

in, when they are pulled up, or when boats drift and anchors drag, coral reefs are damaged. For this reason, permanent moorings are being installed at frequently used dive sites. People can pull up and tie their boats to the permanent, floating mooring buoy. Then the reef is not scarred by anchors over and over again.

Diver Damage   Some coral reefs are damaged directly by divers and snorkelers. The surface of a coral is made up of fragile, living animals. Divers and snorkelers can accidentally kill coral by touching it, standing on it, or kicking their fins against it. Skilled, well-trained divers and snorkelers avoid touching the coral at all.

Overharvesting   Some fish, corals, and other products can be harvested from coral reefs without significant damage. But reefs are under increasing pressure because of the demand for products of various kinds. On some coral reefs, popular food items, such as spiny lobsters and groupers, are being overharvested and have become scarce. Sea cucumbers are harvested in huge numbers near Costa Rica for sale in China and Japan. Black coral has now become rare because so much has been used to make jewelry and carvings. And the harvest of fish for the aquarium/pet industry has been extremely damaging to coral reef communities.

Nuclear Testing   For years, the testing of nuclear bombs was banned by many countries worldwide. Efforts were underway to try to work out a permanent treaty to ban such tests. But negotiations broke down. Beginning in 1995, the French government resumed testing nuclear weapons by blowing up remote coral reefs in the South Pacific. These reefs contain some of the most diverse animal life in the world. The physical destruction of the reefs plus the radioactive contamination from the bombs are both of great concern. Citizens of many countries worldwide protested the destruction of these coral reefs. In 1996, when the French finished the series of tests they had planned, they promised to sign on to the treaty and not do any more tests.

CONSERVATION PROFILE: THE FLORIDA KEYS

In the Florida Keys and south Florida, people are banding together to save nearby coral reefs. Environmental groups are working for better treatment of sewage and other pollution that trickles underground and flows out to the reefs. Recently, offshore oil drilling was banned near the Keys, at least until 2002. And currently, much of the reef is protected in the Florida Keys National Marine Sanctuary, established in 1990.

Because the Florida Keys are such a popular tourist spot, even the protected reefs are in danger of being damaged by so many visitors. To reduce damage, the National Oceanic and Atmospheric Administration and volunteers have installed hundreds of moorings, where people can tie

• SOMETHING'S FISHY IN THE •
AQUARIUM INDUSTRY

Every day, more and more people are keeping colorful reef fish, anemones, and corals in saltwater aquariums. The aquarium trade is a $1 billion-a-year business in the United States. A small number of reef fish are bred in captivity for sale. Some species of clown fish, angelfish, gramma, and cardinal fish are captive bred. But the overwhelming majority of the fish kept in saltwater aquariums are taken from the wild. Coral reefs near Indonesia, the Philippines, Australia, the Bahamas, and Mexico are common collecting sites.

You'd think there would be enough fish in the ocean for people to keep a few as pets. After all, most fish reproduce in large numbers. But fish collecting, as it is now done, is very damaging to fish and coral reefs. For every one fish that arrives at a pet store alive, an estimated twenty or so others died during capture and transport. Given these terrible odds, it's clear that fish collecting is a serious threat to coral reef fish.

Many of these fish are captured by spraying cyanide—a poison—in the water. The poison kills about three-fourths of the fish it contacts. The remaining fish are stunned by the cyanide, making them easy to catch. But meanwhile, the cyanide poisons the corals, killing the reef where the fish live. Another common capture technique is to dynamite a reef, to scare the fish out of their hiding places. Both these techniques kill coral reefs and many of their inhabitants.

Many fish caught by using cyanide die in the pet store or soon after they are taken home. Cyanide poisoning interferes with a fish's nervous system. The fish may look perfectly healthy, but when it is stressed, which occurs when it is bumped or moved, the fish can go into convulsions, lose its buoyancy, and die.

In Southeast Asia, where most reef fish are caught, using cyanide to catch fish is widely banned. But it still goes on. Ironically, cyanide not only poisons the reef, it also burns, sickens, or kills some of the fishermen who use it. Cyanide fishing is also used to catch fish that are shipped to Hong Kong and eaten.

In recent years, people have been purchasing "live rock" from pet stores. Live rock is pieces of the coral reef that are covered with invertebrates or other small animals. These rocks help aquarists set up an aquarium environment where fish, tube worms, corals, sponges, and other reef animals can survive. Live rock is harvested from reefs throughout the world. Aquarium hobbyists argue that the damage to reefs caused by harvesting live rock is negligible, but conservationists disagree. So many tons of coral were harvested from Florida's reefs that the state government took action, banning the collecting of live rock from Florida reefs. Live rock is still available from other reef areas, however, and conservationists are working to encourage governments in those areas to enact bans similar to Florida's.

The saltwater aquarium trade has a long way to go to reduce its negative impact on coral reefs. But some people are working to solve the problem. People are beginning to breed more marine fish in captivity. Steve Robinson, a professional fish collector from the United States, is training fishermen in the Philippines. He is teaching them techniques to catch fish without using cyanide. Other people are working on ways to certify fish as cyanide-free so that fish dealers in the United States can buy fish that are less sickly and that were collected in ways that do not damage reefs. Some day these efforts may make for healthier fish at home *and* healthier fish in the ocean.

up their boats instead of dropping anchors, which can damage the coral. They are also working to improve channel markings so that boat operators will know where to go and their boats will not run aground on coral reefs.

Reef Relief is an environmental group spearheading many reef-conservation efforts in the Keys. It distributes brochures to teach visitors how to snorkel and dive without damaging coral reefs. One of its programs documents the health of the reef with photographs taken through the years. Its Reef Ranger program encourages boat operators of all kinds to report grounded boats, illegal harvest of coral, damaged buoys, and other problems. One person reported someone illegally harvesting coral; the culprit was later caught at the airport, trying to ship the coral for sale!

Each year, Reef Relief, other community groups, and volunteers band together to clean up shorelines in the Florida Keys and south Florida. It is a real community event. Waste companies donate trucks to carry the garbage to landfills. What trash is found on the beaches? Everything from aluminum cans to plastic bags, fishing gear, roofing shingles, and even lawn chairs have been collected!

Those who care about the coral reefs of the Florida

Beach cleanups can benefit coral reefs just offshore.

Keys still have many challenges ahead. Bleaching and coral diseases are becoming more noticeable on parts of the reefs. Sewage from the fast-growing Florida Keys is causing overgrowth of algae, which is covering and killing corals at many reefs. Underwater visibility has decreased from 100 to 150 feet (30 to 45 meters) in the 1970s to less than 50 feet (15 meters) today. Still, the Florida Keys has beautiful reefs and many people who care about them. Tourism related to the coral reefs is a $2 billion-a-year business in the Keys. People who love the reef and depend on it for their livelihood are eager to see these coral reefs thrive.

JELLYFISH GELATIN

The more people know about coral reefs, the better chance coral reefs will be conserved. Help educate others by making a presentation on coral reefs to your friends, family, classmates, or younger students. To add extra fun to your presentation, bring along jellyfish gelatin!

Materials you'll need:
- Two packets of instant gelatin (Choose two different colors. Yellow, blue, or pink work well.)
- A shallow bowl
- A tray or wide pan with sides
- Water
- Saucepan
- Spoon
- Stove
- Spatula
- Butter knife
- Plate

1. Prepare one gelatin packet according to the directions. (You may need an adult's help while working at the stove and when pouring the hot liquid.) Pour the liquid into a bowl. Put the gelatin into the refrigerator to set.

2. Prepare the second packet of gelatin and pour it out into a shallow tray. The gelatin layer should be approximately ¾ inch (2 centimeters) deep. Put it into the refrigerator to set.

3. When the gelatins are set, turn the bowl-shaped gelatin over onto the center of a plate. Remove the bowl. This will be the body of your jellyfish.

4. Use the butter knife to cut the tray of gelatin into long, wavy strips.

5. Using a spatula, transfer the strips to the plate. Arrange the wavy "tentacles" all around the jellyfish's body.

6. Now serve it up—to the disgust and delight of your family or classmates!

Why use gelatin? Sea anemones, corals, and jellyfish all have soft, jellylike bodies. Their flesh has a texture similar to gelatin. Gelatin also has a special ocean connection: one of its ingredients is carageenan, an extract of seaweed!

In some parts of the world, people do eat raw jellyfish. But it must be prepared just right. You and your diners will be much safer trying jellyfish gelatin instead.

For other models of other coral reef residents, try these suggestions:

- For sea urchins, make cheese balls or peanut butter balls and stick toothpicks in them.
- For sea anemones, make cupcakes and insert halves of Gummi Worms in the top to serve as tentacles.
- Make cookies in the shape of sea stars.

Or, think up some other fun reef foods to serve after your presentation. Just let your imagination roam!

MORE CONSERVATION EFFORTS

The Florida Keys is not the only place people are working to conserve coral reefs. Similar efforts have popped up all over the globe:

- In Guam, kids have started a "Kids for Coral" group, which works to save their coral reefs.
- Oman, a country on the Arabian Sea, has made up a conservation plan for its entire reef area and has set aside areas for marine parks.
- Off the southwest tip of Baja California, Mexico, are Las Islas Revillagigedos, a group of islands that attracts scuba divers eager to see its fine reefs, its famous orange angelfish, and giant manta rays. A ban on commercial fishing and large boat traffic within 12 miles (19.4 kilometers) of the islands is helping to preserve this magnificent habitat.
- In Cozumel, Mexico, a cartoon is being used to educate people about coral reefs. "Pepe the Polyp" is the main character!
- The government of Indonesia created the Bunaken Marine Preserve in 1989 to preserve reefs off the coast of North Sulawesi.
- Low-flying aircraft help park rangers protect the 134,300 square miles (349,180 square kilometers) of the Great Barrier Reef Marine Park in Australia. Park managers are drawing up long-term plans for the future of the park. In some parts of the park, fishing is banned and only snorkeling and diving are allowed.
- In Japan, people campaigned to stop the building of an airport that would destroy one of Japan's last remaining undamaged coral reefs. Although the airport is being built, the plans were scaled down due to local and international protests.

• HOPEFUL IN PALAU •

When marine biologist Dr. Robert Johannes set out to learn about coral reefs, he did it in an unusual way. He did not start an experiment or net any fish. Instead, he first talked to Ngiraklang, an eighty-year-old fisherman. Ngiraklang lived in a group of islands called Palau, in the Pacific Ocean, east of the Philippines. What Johannes learned from Ngiraklang were the answers to many questions that had puzzled scientists for years. Ngiraklang and the other expert fishermen had known the answers all along.

Ngiraklang knew when fish gathered on the reef to spawn, according to certain cycles of the moon. He knew the way the fish behaved, and where they could be caught most easily. By watching seabirds feeding on the ocean's surface, he could tell what kind of fish were down below. He was an expert on fish, the way few people will ever be. Often, it is local people such as Ngiraklang who know the most about reefs. People who spend their lives fishing and gathering mollusks from a reef are among the first to recognize the signs that a reef is in trouble ecologically. They are also the people who are willing to care for the reef, partly because they depend on it for their survival.

That is one of the reasons that lately conservationists have changed their approach to conserving reefs, rain forests, and other biomes. Decades ago, a government might just establish a park, kick local people out, and no longer let them use the area. This made local people angry and gave them little reason to protect and care about the park. Today, when a park is established, conservationists try to get local people involved. They try to make sure people benefit from tourism in the park. In addition, special areas often are set aside where local people can hunt, fish, and gather plants.

In the case of coral reefs, some of the best conservation

efforts do not involve parks at all. In many places, national governments are turning control of the reefs over to the local chief of a village or tribe. The local people manage the reefs. They may set aside some areas for fishing, and some areas with no fishing, where the fish can reproduce undisturbed. Studies have shown that fishing improves near areas that are set aside for protection. In the preserves, fish reproduce and spread out to repopulate other areas.

Even if local people know what is best for the future, it may not be easy to change their use of the reef. When someone is offering high prices for fish or shells, it can be hard to turn them down. Politics can complicate change as well. And some islanders' lifestyles have changed so much that they know very little about the reef, unlike their grandparents, who knew a lot. Still, in many cases, turning control of the reefs over to local people seems to work.

In Palau, the old fisherman Ngiraklang has passed away. But other islanders who care about the coral reefs are taking steps to protect them for the future. Two tribal chiefs banned fishing of grouper—a large, popular food fish—during the months when the grouper reproduce. This is expected to help the grouper population, which had drastically declined, to recover. Greenpeace, an international conservation organization, has trained local community members to install permanent reef mooring buoys, which eliminate anchor damage to reefs. The Nature Conservancy, a United States conservation group, is also helping the people of Palau manage their reefs.

So far, conservation efforts are working well. But Palau's reefs are so beautiful, scuba divers are beginning to flock there. Major tourist resorts are being planned for the future. The challenge will be to let people see and enjoy the reefs but still keep the reefs healthy and intact.

- In 1992, representatives from countries all over the world met at the International Convention for the Prevention of Pollution from Ships, also called MARPOL. They strengthened international laws to help prevent the dumping of garbage, toxic waste, plastic, and other pollutants in coastal waters. The new legislation makes it illegal for ships to throw overboard any oil, sewage, toxic chemicals, or garbage close to shore. It also bans disposal of plastics anywhere in the ocean.
- In 1989 Mexico established the Sian Ka'an Biosphere Reserve, which contains rain forests, mangrove swamps, beaches, and coral reefs. Local fishermen are allowed to harvest spiny lobsters in some areas, while other areas are entirely protected. Tourism is being slowly and carefully developed.

The varied and creative efforts to save coral reefs give people hope that these habitats will be conserved for the future. But more people are needed to help with reef-saving efforts worldwide. Even if you do not live near a coral reef, you can get involved in saving these unique habitats. For tips on what you can do, read the next section.

RESOURCES AND WHAT
YOU CAN DO TO HELP

Here's what you can do to help ensure that coral reefs are conserved:

• Learn more by reading books and watching videos and television programs about coral reefs. Check your local library, bookstore, and video store for resources. Here are just a few of the books available for further reading:

Caribbean Reef Ecology by William S. Alevizon (Pisces Books, 1994).

Coral Reef: A City That Never Sleeps by Mary E. Cerullo (Cobblehill, 1996).

Coral Reefs by Dwight Holing (Silver Burdett Press, 1995).

Coral Reefs: Earth's Undersea Treasures by Laurence Pringle (Simon & Schuster, 1995).

The Greenpeace Book of Coral Reefs by Sue Wells and Nick Hanna (Sterling Publishing Company, 1992).

Oceans, The Illustrated Library of the Earth edited by Robert E. Stevenson, Ph.D., and Frank H. Talbot, Ph.D. (Rodale Press, 1993).

The Random House Atlas of the Oceans edited by Dr. Danny Elder and Dr. John Penetta (Random House, 1991).

- To explore oceans through your computer, check your local computer store for these interactive CD-ROMs:

Cities Under the Sea: Coral Reefs, Enteractive (Distributed by Enteractive, Phone 1-800-452-9999).

Coral Reef!: The Vanishing Undersea World, Arnowitz Studios (Distributed by Maxis, Phone 1-800-33-MAXIS).

Microsoft Oceans (Distributed by Ingram, Phone 1-800-937-8000).

- For more information on conservation issues related to coral reefs, contact the following organizations:

American Oceans Campaign
725 Arizona Avenue, Ste. 102
Santa Monica, CA 90401
Phone 1-310-576-6162

Center for Marine Conservation
1725 DeSales Street, NW
Washington, DC 20036
Phone 1-202-429-5609
(They cover all ocean issues, especially plastic pollution, and help manage coastal cleanups worldwide.)

Greenpeace USA
1436 U Street NW
Washington, DC 20009
Phone 1-202-462-1177

Reef Relief
P.O. Box 430
Key West, FL 33041
Phone 1-305-294-3100
(This coral reef conservation organization has an environmental center and store located at 201 William Street, in Key West, Florida. They also have a program you can access on the World Wide Web at http: www//Florida-Keys.FL.US. If you would like to be a "Sea Fan," an offical member of Reef Relief, the cost is $20 per year. The membership fee covers quarterly newsletters, a bumper sticker, a membership decal, action alerts, and other membership mailings.)

If you like the job these organizations are doing, consider becoming a member.

- Improve coral reef habitat by participating in Coastal Cleanups each fall. For information on beach cleanups in your area, contact the Center for Marine Conservation at the address and phone number above. Or, organize your own beach cleanup, any day of the year!

- Work to reduce your use of plastics that may end up in the marine environment. Plastic bags, ropes, bottles, and other items can kill wildlife. When you go to a store, bring cloth bags, old paper bags, or old plastic bags. Use these bags instead of getting new bags each trip. When you purchase an item, decide whether you really need a bag to carry it. Politely tell the checkout person if you don't need one. (Always carry the receipt for the item with you in case you need to prove you paid for it.) For cloth bags and other environmental products, contact the following company for a catalog:

Seventh Generation
Colchester, VT 05446-1672
Phone 1-800-456-1177

- Work with your family to reduce your use of toxic chemicals that can pollute coastal waters. Many products people use at home and in the yard—cleansers, paints, nail polishes, pesticides, and motor oils—contain toxic ingredients. These chemicals, when dumped on driveways, in streets, down storm drains, or down kitchen sinks, can end up in streams and rivers, which lead to coastal waters. Waste treatment plants usually cannot get all the toxic pollutants out of the water before they release it into streams, bays, and oceans. Check your local library for information on household toxins and alternatives to those toxins. Call your local sanitation department and ask them about household hazardous waste programs in your area. You could also check the following publications for information:

Nontoxic, Natural, and Earthwise by Debra Lynn Dadd (Jeremy P. Tarcher, 1990).
Ranger Rick, April 1988, a special Earth Day issue.

For commercially-prepared alternatives to toxic household products, contact Seventh Generation, listed above, or Real Goods, listed in the entry below.

• Turn off lights, televisions, and other appliances when you are not using them. Reduce unnecessary car trips by walking, bicycling, taking buses, or combining trips. Saving oil and gas and electricity that may be made in power plants, which burn oil and gas, helps prevent the need for the offshore oil drilling and oil transport that can lead to oil spills and other ocean pollution. Encourage your family to use energy-saving devices in your home. For more energy-saving tips, contact your local electric utility. For a catalog of energy-saving appliances and other environmental products, write to:

Real Goods
966 Mazzoni Street
Ukiah, CA 95482-3471
Phone 1-800-762-7325

• Write letters to state and national government officials, telling them you feel coral reef conservation is important.

GLOSSARY

ahermatypic   a coral that does not build reefs

algae   a simple plant that does not have true leaves, stems, or roots

atoll   a ring-shaped coral reef that encloses a lagoon and is surrounded by open ocean

barrier reef   a coral reef parallel to a coastline and separated from it by a lagoon

biome   an area that has a certain kind of community of plants and animals. In the case of terrestrial biomes and coral reef, they have a certain climate as well. In contrast, other aquatic biomes such as lake and stream can occur in many different climates.

bleaching   the process by which a coral polyp ejects its zooxanthellae. This leaves the coral white, appearing bleached.

calcareous algae   algae that cement pieces of coral together, thereby strengthening the coral reef

chromatophore   an animal cell containing pigment

colony   a group of organisms of the same species that live together and depend on one another

commensalism   a partnership between two organisms of different species in which one partner benefits and the other neither benefits nor is harmed

elasmobranch   a class of fish with skeletons made of cartilage. Sharks, rays, and skates are members of this class.

El Niño   a pattern of weather systems that creates a warm current flowing south along the coast of Ecuador.

fringing reef   a coral reef that grows outward from a shoreline

hermatypic   a coral that forms calcium carbonate rapidly enough to help develop reefs

lagoon   shallow area of ocean separated from the open ocean by a reef

mutualism   a relationship between two organisms in which both partners benefit

parasitism   a relationship between organisms in which one organism benefits and the other is harmed

phyla   the highest groupings of animals within the animal kingdom. Scientists group organisms according to the characteristics they share.

phytoplankton   tiny, often microscopic, plants that float in the ocean

plankton   organisms that primarily float along with ocean currents instead of actively swimming

planulae   free-swimming larvae of jellyfish, corals, sea anemones, or hydra

polyp   an individual, soft-bodied, coral animal

reef crest   the highest part of the reef, where waves break

reef flat   the flat or gently sloping area that runs from the beach or lagoon to the crest of the reef

reef front   the front of the reef, facing the open ocean. Also called the fore-reef.

suspension feeder   an animal that eats particles of food suspended—floating through but not dissolved—in water

symbiosis   a relationship between two organisms of different species in which at least one of the two animals benefits

zooxanthellae   algae that live symbiotically within corals

INDEX

PHOTO CREDITS

593.6 Sayre, April Pulley
SAYRE

   Coral reef

                                    11666
$16.98